ROBERT SCHUMANN IS MAD AGAIN

Norman Dubie

COPPER CANYON PRESS
Port Townsend, Washington

Cover art: VJB/Scribe. Image source: *Miscellaneous Manuscript 301.*
Courtesy of the Irving S. Gilmore Music Library, Yale University.

Copper Canyon Press is in residence at Fort Worden State Park in Port
Townsend, Washington, under the auspices of Centrum. Centrum is a
gathering place for artists and creative thinkers from around the world,
students of all ages and backgrounds, and audiences seeking extraor-
dinary cultural enrichment.

LIBRARY OF CONGRESS CATALOGING-IN-PUBLICATION DATA
Names: Dubie, Norman, 1945– author.
Title: Robert Schumann is mad again / poems by Norman Dubie.
Description: Port Townsend, Washington : Copper Canyon Press, [2019]
Identifiers: LCCN 2018048963 | ISBN 9781556595653 (paperback :
     alk. paper)
Subjects: LCSH: American poetry—21st century.
Classification: LCC PS3554.U255 A6 2019 | DDC 811/.54—dc23
LC record available at https://lccn.loc.gov/2018048963

9 8 7 6 5 4 3 2   FIRST PRINTING

COPPER CANYON PRESS
Post Office Box 271
Port Townsend, Washington 98368

www.coppercanyonpress.org

ACKNOWLEDGMENTS

The American Poetry Review: "Delmore Schwartz Vigilant among Large-Headed Lilacs," "Elegy for Brian Young," "Prophecy in Lieu of a Lien," and "Spy."

Blackbird: "Crater Lviv," "Kathmandu," "The Nine Solitary Plasters of a Comedy," "Snowden in Hong Kong" as "Snow Down in Hong Kong," and "Sokurov Thought the City Was Empty."

The Blue Guitar: "Homage to St. Geraud," "In the Choir Loft," "In the Transfers of a Long Beard," and "The Old Women at Urnekloster House."

Bombay Gin: selections from "The Colophons of Solomon" as "The Eight Watery Colophons of Solomon."

ELKE: "Romance."

Empty Mirror: "A Third Scroll of Malachite," with a painting by Joost de Jonge.

The Fiddlehead: "Boston & Maine," "Dementia," "Grasmere, N.H.," "In an Exchange of Many Goodbyes to All That...," and "Vladimir N.'s Bestiary of Flashy Fiction."

Hinchas de Poesia: "An I.R.S. Official from Houston Visits the Blood on a Stone Stylus:," "*NOT A SPAGHETTI MINIMALIST'S SACK / OF WRITS AND CHITS, NOT THE MOVIE WITH A DEAD BEARD IN IT*," and "A Week's Reading of the Newspaper."

Joost de Jonge. *The Convergence: Painted Poetry & Painterly Poetics—an ekphrastic notion* (2016): "The Convergence."

Lake Effect: "Zone."

Memorious: "*La logique assassine*," "Robert Schumann Is Mad Again &," and "Two Eloping Disks with the Same Radius."

Narrative: "December 7, 2015" and "Ghost Writer."

The New Yorker: "Caravaggio, Texas" and "Tucson, Monday Love."

The Pinch: "The Elgar Enigma Repetitions, '33."

The Plume Anthology of Poetry 4: "Nimrod & the Flying Pig."

The Plume Anthology of Poetry 5: "*The pilgrims* above."

The Southeast Review: "Trow Hill, Vermont."

Spillway: "Cloaked in Night, Rising in Radiant Orchard," "Portrait of Donald Trump in a Purple Codpiece," and "The Kingdom."

Waxwing: "scion, *circa* TEN."

In memory of my father, mother, and sister

CONTENTS

ROBERT SCHUMANN IS MAD AGAIN

I

THE OLD WOMEN AT URNEKLOSTER HOUSE

for Dorothy

Heisenberg on his aunts' ceiling
counting the shut-ins. *One*
giving names to individual
tulip bulbs sighing with the fish bones
and red potting soil on wet newsprint,
another, also mathematical,
obsessing on the current sum of pewter spoons,
and the *third* wrapping in wool
a hot teapot her younger sister says
is the color of marmalade custard.

The dog is larger than the rug
he chooses to sleep on
and he's suffering from arthritis.
When he is finally dead the three women
will drag him
down the stairs
on potato sacks they spent
the morning sewing together
as a burial sled.

(The blue clock beside the spring onions
should know how long it took
to arrive at the moment
where suddenly *it* stops
forever but without the usual importance.
However, physically
its perfect enamel face is not self-conscious
like cereal caught in the sergeant's mustache
if his mouth, still worse,

is a black hole and nursery of suns unbelievably
adamant at the center of its universe.)

The fall from one step to the next
releases methane from the dead dog
and Heisenberg thinks this is all
stacked like a model
for reluctant space/time
with a cold flat outcome
for both the dog and the cosmos.

IN THE TRANSFERS OF A LONG BEARD

It is talk between a confused veteran
and the old woman flirting
with certain dementia in the cold fog of a bus stop.

He's saying something about phantoms
of faint pastel, purples and yellow,
vaseline-thin paper sheen on an old stamp
moving low as a smell
on the other blurring side
of the trees: men
who have been shitting on the run
for all of their short lives. *No question.*

And the sergeant will drop
these common fucks
before they make it, in thought
even, to the shade along the dry riverbed.
Wind now and damn hot, *fuck,* is it enough
to add to this
their now rat-tat opened intestines scrolling in the grasses:

this canceling the smell that was
common, something
like cinnamon and boiled cabbages. She frowns.

She snickers: young man
it is the odor of oils, cod musk
on an old exercised dog
steaming in from the warm rainstorm
that is your perfume du jour
and more gloom, than boom-boom.

Boom-boom? I can't reason
with myself
let alone with a hero who mews and chatters
like the deer in my backyard
when, god forbid, it drops way below
zero...

THE KINGDOM

Little Mari asks, softly,
could you write a poem for me
about a princess
who is hanging in a cupboard—
her already ragged dress
is caught on a nail,
it's not that depressing:
a mouse in a bone-china cup
rowing forever toward the princess
saying that *no*
it is depressing, what we
are not told is that the nail
at its tip is white
with poison—can you
please write something like that
so anyone will care enough
to read it?

TUCSON, MONDAY LOVE

She lost her hat in the a.m.—
in front of the Laundromat where she has been unconscious
in the hammock of his narrative
for most of this day—the snake
in the tree above them
was digesting a small deer—
the deer's bones like a ghost ship
blossoming as a mere trick inside a clear bottle—

it now sails past the daymoon on her long bare arm
that she scratches
with the calloused toe
of a croissant, the
coffee is bitter enough. She says
to the colonized moon, to its residential rich,
"I've always hated the traffic in this town—
              its miracle of legumes and fish."

CRATER LVIV

It's the darker side of most everything
and our moon
where Lizardmen have built from silk
and the despised bones of their intellectuals
retaining tanks
with Quonset cribs as seven-dimensional dispatches
for the more feared prisoners.

The pivot in one roof enforced with the leg bones
of a long-dead cosmonaut. There's a great deal
of secrecy about these detainment ponds—
as a first idea they were the brainstorm
of Hans Frank, a Jew-killer
of unusual aptitude, to quote
these Lizardmen slamming tankards of grain alcohol
on their long table of birch. Governor Frank's son

carried a thrice-faded photograph of his hanged father
inside a passport
to grow confidence in the future of humankind.
(Martha confides the son for the most part
was opposed to capital punishment.) The stone doves
when released on this side of the moon
are punctuated with the mass volleying of shotguns.

The gravity of pellets here on our
moon is certainly theoretical and bemused—
like the smudged trains departing *Lviv* for the death camps
at *Lwów.* (Somehow, they are the same place—
please, this is something
you must not share with the more fragile
of the children.)

HOMAGE TO ST. GERAUD

Sometimes believing in the beauty
of the fresh elevated incarnate existences
of the wheel, he wishes instead

for an eternal status, a
stone and fetal sleep
like that of the uncollected dead
under the linen snows on Everest.

CARAVAGGIO, TEXAS

The fire truck edged up onto the sidewalk.
I was smitten with stooping
in the iridescent rhubarb
and with the expected cramping of moon.

I was going philosophical over
the body count in my favorite soaps—
I know when I get bored they kill, *say*,
the librarian-who-stutters just
to ease me through my day.

To be smitten with pain is a discipline,
the priest used to say...
The fire truck looked like a poor man's
meat loaf sweet with ketchup and onions.

The firemen in large downturned boots
walked toward me like dead
commissioners of baseball
looking
for a reddening rib eye in the winter
sunlight—this unusually long winter
of rain...

I loosened my bra with an innocent
adjustment of my left shoulder. These guys
don't shoot down poles anymore, they
miss the bells, too,
but insist they cook their wives
under the table. I said
to the old one, you mean *drink*
them under the table. *I wish*

was his response, eyeing
my neighbor's ass and the smoke
pouring from the garage—I had set
yellow rags on fire
with a magnifying glass. If you'll
believe this, it accompanied my ex-husband's

favorite dictionary,
which he abandoned
when he ran off with Jolienne,
my sister's second baby, not really
just out of the carriage, but from
what I would describe
as her most memorable marriage.

A THIRD SCROLL OF MALACHITE

circa AD 800

The magus as a small boy in Egypt
in his faded linens
thought that the torchlight reflected in the harbor
was a simple exchange of sleeping gulls
over their sea of salt— a dark disk in the sky
believed the other brother
resented the elders in the cliffs' cavities
because their birds and scales full of dry bread
were both blackened. The serpent

offering quinces like stadia tickets to the women,
just a joke about the boats in the sky
resembling the green scudding clouds of the sea.

The winter chorus of martyred infants
sings with hesitation.
So, the cry of the gull is torchlight
climbing over the wharves at midnight. This is a sleight
of mind and some hillside soliloquy saying
there will be sweet figs threaded
there where inside the seed
yet another seed is nesting like some Roman poison
in the wine of a country wedding.

Here, tacking the sincere jewels
of the pomegranate substitutes for golden
songbirds in trees. The mother dreaming
of a new Jerusalem with tilting sticks on a hill.
They purposefully wield her young son
through the colored garden
where the sleeves collect
like cold waters in a stone fountain.

More gulls snoring up inside
the young master's dress that is folded jade
like an ocean with buttons of bone and alabaster
alternately...

                                    up in the branches of olive
the wind whispers...   do not touch me
for I have not yet descended, I am
the old sun that will kiss you on both cheeks
repeatedly, with an extra scent of solemnity, the full
daymoon now dressed but shoeless...

                                    like a kind whore
she calls us to her breasts
which are labeled opalescent rubbish. *Now, please,*
be well for less with more.

IN THE CHOIR LOFT

The snow collapsed the slate roof
as if in boxes. Dark birds
lifting in the last sifted flour of it.
The blazing egg tempera of a night mural
representing the winter comets
of a lost century: brook trout of icy tails
and then the solemn ashes in heaps
with more snow
over the Communion table—its good leg
is a dozen leather-bound concordances. The goat
sleeping in the low cupboard with candles
had suffocated in the smoke. Its body now
a larger fraction of snow, wax, and more smoke.

The leaning workhorses from Quebec
brought down the north wall
of fieldstone, the giant crucifix
launched almost across the frozen pond.

The priest in his nightshirt
holding a single candle. He had started
the fire while boiling eggs or coffee?
He wasn't certain, his mind
abandoned him in his early sixties.
He blamed the fat nun
from Nova Scotia. He once
loved her. The white mole on the neck.
She simply laughs at him. Her ghost
standing under the horse chestnut tree
down by the dock. She had
passed with the comets. The heated bell

had broken through the ice
and settled at the bottom of the pond. The horses
that pulled down the wall
would drag the cold bell from the water
in early April. Its tongue

was never, ever found. He finally confessed
he was boiling eggs,
which was unseemly for an old priest,
when the gas jets in the kit
flooded there in the dumb light of what,
he allowed,
was a new morning without forgiveness.

He was called Father L'Dieu and the kids adored
him; late in the interview
with the news crew from Montreal, he smiled
adding that the Sisters of Mercy
were a pack of depraved whores.

He was sucking on the icicle
he said was restored to him
from the poor box.

He gave them all the middle digit
and walked off with a urinal
spilling a heavy cream—he'd milked
the cow in the shed
and someone now screamed
that it too was burning.

He threw the milk at it.

PORTRAIT OF DONALD TRUMP IN A PURPLE CODPIECE

circa 1592

The wardens of the early morning
throw off their cloaks and wooden shoes.

A line of cypress is fanning
the obese clouds.

The merchant's pink fight-dogs
run the horizon, save the largest one

who is smelling around the feet
of the silent hen-mistress with an apron's

hammock of speckled eggs that must
be washed and then polished repeatedly...

In a short nap that afternoon
she will bleed from the eyes and die twice.

She dared nibble at her lord's marbled
cake weighted in strawberries with clear sleeves

of pear. The lord expressing his gratitude
while freeing bees with smoke

beside her open grave. The new cooks
still dancing sideways

in the slanting rain and trees.

NIMROD & THE FLYING PIG

1

The king was burning the tall grasses
to market an exhaust, a gate
animals would spring from, Nimrod's
archers dropping them in air,
in service to the autumn banquet.

It felt nearly a winter's day and the king
looked into the black smoke of the sky
while a green flying sow
passed wildly overhead detailing
to the king that he was shameless
and truly cursed among men.

2

This pig threw this king off his need
for a harvest mead. He returned
a large cart full of grapes and wheat
to his old toothless mother

3

whom he had imprisoned months earlier
somewhere in the southern swamp.

4

Nimrod began to fast. He shaved
his head and snorted myrrh with prayers.
Then the pig flew over again, over

Nimrod's bathhouse,
which was open to sky.

The pig told the king once more
that essentially
he was doomed beyond remedy,

more than anyone who'd lived in recorded history.
(This limitation, its specificity
with reference to time, emboldened

Nimrod who reached instantly for his bow, piercing
mortally the pig's throat
with a long yellow arrow of pine wood.)

    5

From that day forward the king
lived in perfect happiness
far into old age
and was blessed with six sons
who like their father were also cruel
beyond definition.

The king said he was individually
charmed among men. Reports,
in fact, insist that his mother is still
living in a suburb of Annapolis—

'flying pig' is N.S.A.
code for something you'd *seriously*
rather not know. Now,

read our poem to its conclusion
but never tell a single living soul
of your exposure to it.

Oh, and
the pig's name was Protobus.

Protobus is an anagram
of Hamlet. Thelma is an anagram
of Hamlet. Pity the poor pig.
Poor all of us.

ODE

What is it about the train's passing...   *what is it?*

A WEEK'S READING OF THE NEWSPAPER

April 30, 2016

Colonel Richthofen sucking sauce off ribs
worries that the condor's blue shadow
is on his ceiling again, glass snippets
of morphine broken on the floor
with the dead carpenter's bare lightbulb
showing images of Luftwaffe plucking
from the firestorm the very lungs
of the children of Guernica—   then, of course,
Picasso in gaslight smuggling gold
for the Germans.
Paint ain't costly, Ma, is it?
One potato, two potato, three…
Ma?
Xi's homage to Mao is an eccentricity!
Ma?
The shadows of the camels on the mud wall
suggested sea monsters to my daughter—
James Baldwin telling her this is a certain predictor
of a future violence. He was seen
eating soiled carrots in Provence. (The smoke of *gernika*
leaving his very precise ears.) Suddenly in the overview, a red ceiling
fan and a pig reading a catalogue
remind my daughter of the polar bear
eating a vanilla ice-cream cone
on a slowly watched train.
The bear is a wax effigy with a spasmodic
inner radiance; its stained
ass is like cubes of ice in a glass of scotch.
Richthofen sipping there!
It is of course tragic that my daughter
and I have spoken twice in five months. The giant
Virgin in Piero's scarlet cassock,

wings spread,
balancing a bowl of grapes
on her head. In Rimini,
they think nothing of noble solids of geometry
detailing a woman who squats to pee...
a fair-skinned boy, Piero remarked, is leading the darkness
down the long hall, all four hands also
very white and small.
Piero saying it is something
I can never forgive my father for having done.
Something he shouldn't have, not
to his own son. Then
there is a detail that is missing...
one potato, two potato, Ma.

II

ROBERT SCHUMANN IS MAD AGAIN &

mother is dead.
What of the requiem wood,
the requiem grasses?

No one explained, the
stomach calls
in empty loon voices
over the pond
as you fall
forever toward the water. Exactly, mother
is dead.

At the requiem breakfast
Schumann is mad again.

I had expected less...

DIALOGUE OF THE ONE AND ZERO

for Laura

Mother whispered, she should *friend*
her dead brother because one
of our two snow stations
up in the mountain's notch, the oldest
one, in fact, was burned down
by starving vagrants. Firemen

running in snowshoes chased
the three bearded men through pine wood
into the back of a small hardware store
and into the neighboring pharmacy,
passing two teenagers ogling one another
beside a machine full of cold Coke...
then, they vanished in plain view
of even the modern security video. Is this
the pilgrim's miraculous
slough of despond?
The storefront alarms were very loud.

She said, *further, I'm relieved. We'll never*
truly understand
that they were desperate and meant
us no real harm—no one listens to me,

but we need to begin
to cool our poor human brains. I'm telling you
we're getting really strange all over again.
The last time it was like this, children,

it was war, and then war again.
Practically everyone starved...

THE ELGAR ENIGMA REPETITIONS, '33

So I say to the composer's tin triangle:
what disturbs me
is the intolerant nun
who said, "until these outer gifts—storytelling
and imagination
and all the emotions that attend them—
are silenced or dragged
into submission
to our union with our Lord, until then
we cannot come to perfect realization.

Further, all you artists are children..."

Sister, I say, the Warsaw streets
with their sinister trees are now speaking
about the coming horror,
speaking in the many strange voices of something
like a volleying tennis ball...
alien and preposterous, it is singing to nearly
everyone who will listen. And to

nearly no one of importance.

Light in the ghetto houses' windows
might be fire, could be an amber
streetlamp, and in this hour
of obvious error,
the children are listening,
the children who care
by definition,
who are a melody of instruction without fear,
all of them solemn, deliberate and minor

to the meaning of the meaning
of the occasion or air, oxygen
or music from broken paper accordions

spread out over the cobbled streets, everywhere.

SOKUROV THOUGHT THE CITY WAS EMPTY

My thought *was* water is light in carriage, fire
heavy in its digestion.
She asked me about the dead cops in Parkland Hospital.
I said Chekhov and Auden both died alone in the same hotel
in Berlin? Or Brussels?
They knew the bubbles in the bath
were the fossilization of their snoring. The ghost
of a dead President whispering that a country having practiced
slavery will suffer thousands of years of lousy karma. The
Greeks still throwing chunks of polished marble at their police.
Scalia dead under his pillow in a hunting lodge in Texas
thought racism was just a lost nostalgia for the novels
of Sir Walter Scott. *Alexandre, it was summer*
and the hour for reading books to children.
Dallas making the ones who weren't listening
carefully into orphans. The nurses making a painted screen
from Baghdad of their bodies—privacy, a dignity for the corpses
even though they didn't require it of them. John Wayne clipping
his toenails in the Alamo looks up and gives Wolf Blitzer
the middle finger. I never said I was a common intellectual.
The sort the Germans in Poland hanged from lampposts. The sallow
filmmaker saying that *Europe is everywhere.* What a crisis, mostly
of languages. And the executioner's daughter-in-law is drinking
water from a tin cup
trembling a little at her lips. They read books
to her written mostly in Russian. Here the city
is also empty and for cannibalism to work they relied
on the drifting snow for refrigeration. *Alexandre, your film left*
me sorrowful. A distant voice on the radio saying huge rocks
were slamming into the earth. The sniper high in the parking lot
runs down in boredom to kill another officer,
 neither of them

gives a damn about the mass extinction that makes a fossil
of a fish in sand in Morocco, a string of shit intact still leaving
the dead fish millions of years ago. The sand is orange. *The city
is empty*. The fish is irritable. The snow is piling up
at the doorstep.

STORM

for W.D.

When a wall of dust is entering the city
the old copper hood over the stove gets nervous, the damper
increasingly nervous,
flopping about,
while the sand moves nearer to the house.

The death of friends approaches,
paced but nearly relentless, again like that tin damper
seizing in its narrow brick exhaust. Another lover

has died; once she edged across the room
saying she wanted
the heat off the acid I'd taken
inside her as well.

Our friend
Ellen had committed suicide six months before.
She said eventually
she believed the dying of old friends
would become serial, frantic. She thought that,

while wiping up between her legs. Then she said
no, not like that... forget please
I ever said it.

BOSTON & MAINE

The salt marsh at sunset, something
of a carved rosewood landscape
for an early 20th century toy train set
that's left the mountain's tunnel,
the smoke of the woodbox
darkening everything in the heavy
mix with steam, the men's faces of ivory
washed in the ink. Leaving the mountain,
the eyes of the children in the sleeper
opened again. The conductor
chuckled. A horse
in the mail carriage screamed.

This woke the stationmaster
who looked at his wife, saying,
it is the 2:11—3hrs late. She
smiles, "Darling, I'm not
sure that we've ever formally
met?" He quickly removes his hand from her hair.
She wakes. The train edges
under a water tower. The paper birds
on the salt marsh are lifting
into the night's stars under the very soft rain.

AN I.R.S. OFFICIAL FROM HOUSTON VISITS THE BLOOD ON A STONE STYLUS:

for C.

Marcus, I hope you like these two postcards:
the three heaps of pastel sheep manure
                              are not an azure I consider
adequate to the browning of sunlight,
but the green lawns *are,* and to be
here at Palenque with Mayan gardeners
seated on their broad gasoline mowers
is just such a thrill, Charlie bribed
something like a justice of peace
and grounds-warden's wife

                    and so I explained,
dear Charlie, my third eye sees
the cactus thorn lifted off a blue leaf
by the jaguar priest—
he pierces the foreskin of the prince
and then individually the dowager-mother's labia,
again I mean as if aspects
of a single roiling leaf, glistening in morning mist...

an agate bull that is green collects the blood,
the two donations.   The aristocrats are bored sitting
in the strong sun... the blood
is mixed with mortar for a cornerstone
devoted to the chapelette
in the glade where the granddaughter drowned
under an enormous day moon... Charlie

distracts me saying the tuna sandwiches are dry, need
more *mayonnaise and mustard...* he says
the lawns are still too wet for mowing, all

the ghosts, at noon,
laughing at us. I tell Charlie to ignore them,
if they had ever tasted mustard on their fish
they wouldn't find us so ludicrous...

And Charlie said, bet your sweet ass, babe.

ROMANCE

A gray plate of steaming mussels
and a draught saucer
of butter with floating slivers of garlic—
Van Gogh coughs an affirmation
at his brother who puts
his brown cigarette on the edge of the table—
he walks down
the long street. He entered
the rain, leaving the green awning.
Each passing second they are
somewhat more distant. They're
both infected with syphilis.
Theo is visiting his new girlfriend. She is
not suffering with his infection.

He gives her a dripping wet
bouquet of stolen calamus.
In fact, Theo thinks
she is still a virgin. She isn't.
In less than a decade they all are
dead and buried. The two brothers
believe in the superstition
of posterity. Her syphilis actually
was congenital. As of last April
all of them were entirely virginal.
They do remain my best and only
imaginary friends. I like
a feint of mustard with my mussels.
I like the rain.

the sickly-green successive ribbing with tangerine arcseconds
in the night tunnel—fumes and the headlights flickering against
the staggered watch-boxes, blue with enamel sheeting. Your skirt
hiked up, a pint of scotch with a sanitary napkin, half a doughnut—
you thought that Nietzsche, Lou Andreas-Salomé, and Rilke
got lost walking in southern Russia. They had shared a hayloft
the night before with rain. A rain that was pure vinegar with
the ecstasy of simple feasting on pickles and cheese, the laughter
of Rilke urinating down on the white horses… the nettle-rose deciding
then and there to kill him with the simple prick of nitrogen,
a sepsis of the blood. Lou eating scrambled pheasant eggs off hot slate.
Friedrich finishing his cheese and dried plums smiles and says
bite me. Composte. Compadre. Calumny. Cunt. Chuckle. Catastrophe.
Then fewer and fewer uncorrupted witnesses. Mr. Terrance.
These 19th century bosses are munching irritably on salted popcorn
while watching your lengthy movie, *The Night of Broken Teacups*,
yes, that's right, with glee what he had said was *you can bite me.*

NOT A SPAGHETTI MINIMALIST'S SACK / OF WRITS AND CHITS, NOT THE MOVIE WITH A DEAD BEARD IN IT

after Tarantino

His sister's half cousin
with frothy breasts comes in from the tennis court
and is thinking his last movie suffered an embargo of cops
and uniformed *what-nots*, she thought
to herself that the gratuitous blood
just this once was enigmatic like the two drying
ropes of chinese noodles that ran from the station house
through a mountain snowstorm to an outer barn
as well as to a logically distant outhouse, all
of it / invisible closets of shit in a white blindness.

Yet the cop in seattle snuck into the matinee / because
last night he woke from the same fucking dream
where a *chick*, all of thirteen, empties a silver pistol
into his lower spine. She spits on the dark sidewalk
where a pond of blood / supports
a dozen skaters, some falling
to their bottoms startled at *that*,
not to mention *at* the dying cop
who is holding desperately the rope
staggering / out into a blinding wilderness of snow smelling / equally
of horses and the hairy asses of the men who drive them
toward a nothingness of schedules
without destinations, moral or otherwise...
you know, like trawlers out at sea
disfigured and arbitrary with the sunset.

DEMENTIA

Uccello was one of the old painters whom the Abbot
scolded for fields colored blue and massive clouds
bright green in a terrible wind. My mother stuttering,
I'm going to say goodnight to you and go
to the boardwalk with our dead aunt. She also once painted
a red ox standing next to a small girl in a torn dress.

She said, the Abbot was trying to poison Uccello
with simple cheese. She repeated, in hushed terms to me,
that living outside Florence,
if you had learned to drive an automobile,
life truly would have been a living hell. But
I love you, son. Happy Christmas. & let us know how
that turns out for you?

You know, I just can't stand those nosy, opinionated
priests. Did you know the word 'amen' has its origin
in some vulgar sun-worshipping Egyptian king: boo-hoo, crazy
Akhenaten. I think?
They killed him dead,
chopped him up and fed him to the black crocodiles
in the formerly milk-white river. Priests! And a small
torn dress, you know, one that would
be appropriate for summer mornings...

III

IN AN EXCHANGE OF MANY GOODBYES TO ALL THAT...

for J.

I listen to a woman on TV
talking about North Korea.
I leave the room
for the balcony and watch an old dog
crossing under the trees, a flock
of pigeons rises to the roof, a small blue
feather falling through air—

the dog barks twice in open conflict
with the feather
that settles on the grass
that's green like the nested hair
of an easter basket...
he looks up at me embarrassed.

I say, *that was good work.*
He smiles broadly and trots
on down the street. What
could possibly be wrong with the world.

We must know—*please*
let us begin with the interrogation of pigeons.

GRASMERE, N.H.

for my brother

The slanting rain of yellow contretemps
and ordinary evenings on the river
with apples, fresh garlic, and two jars
of purple jam. A heel of bread, burnt
like pepper in the cooling house.
Then waking in the chair to
your own sudden face in night glass
in a south window.

The last bird flies by... You're happy
you've said your goodbyes
to the cat who's now
just a shadow up the stairs. The farther
ghost coming to the piano
in the kitchen—the black lacquered radio
of your grandfather.

The constellations are warping at the horizon.
It will happen in your sleep, please.
More and colder rain—
Bach's quick tin again receding
with the littlest feet
while something else like the red gate is opening...
on a memory you've been subtracted from deliberately...

VLADIMIR N.'S BESTIARY OF FLASHY FICTION

I smelled lilacs. The semester was over. This was
a second night with a woman still
very strange to me. I'd suffered a nosebleed
that morning. I could smell lilacs. I was certain
the frogs in her firepond were almost intelligent.
I whispered to her that the frogs were a spooky
summary of watery ovation. In a raised voice she angrily asked
if I meant to encourage them? Then in a new quite
pleasant voice she wondered if I could now eat anything?
I responded with such emphasis that the frogs in the pond,
in a sudden battery, went silent on me. I said, I could
eat a possum whole. She flinched, I think, and began
to recite a fragment from Eliot's "Journey of the Magi."
I left her, to drink some scotch on the porch.
I left her smiling while sautéing garlic and onions.
I nearly shared with her the fact that the brilliant
Eliot scholar, Matthew Groton Bate, could not be given
a much-deserved House at Harvard because that would
require his students calling him Master Bate. I thought better of it.
I smelled the white lilacs. Time passed. Drunk, needing more ice,
I joined her in the blue walk-in cupboard
where I was confronted with bits of hair and then just
the small wet head of a young possum with startled eyes, it
nevertheless seemed to be caught yawning. Briefly, I thought
of it as an oracle. I was trying, I believe, to formalize
something quite impossible. But really it did seem to me
to be about to say something famously. I shared this
with Elizabeth—she then with no ceremony began to remove
her shirt and red bra, saying the left breast tells
the future; the right, the past. I remember swallowing
saliva. She frowned in the silence and said that an old man,
in a little-known poem—an old, bent man crossed over

Niagara Falls on a taut wire while his toothless lion
in a wheelbarrow was roaring out in the familiar
cri de coeur of lions. But the anxious gathered tourists
and newlyweds could not hear him over the also
roaring falls and they just concluded that the lion yawned.
She added that dinner, dripping with a yellow raisin gravy,
was never a pet, was in fact fattened to a purpose but was not familiar
with the anecdote about the lion. So I spoke immediately to
the pendulous right breast, saying timidly,
then it's not playing possum. I was for the first time in years
forming a new theory about human misunderstandings. The other
breast answered me with yet another quotation
from verse. Something about going down a mountain
with your uncle on a heavily waxed toboggan. While she recited,
I was naturally thinking of doing the police in voices.
I was understandably dressing myself in a second condom.
Somehow, again, the frogs went silent. She said I should think
of them, as a community, as mostly polymorphous-perverse. *Norman
        O. Brown,*
she whispered. With that, I came all over myself
and the cat I had taken until then for shadow. The cat's
complaint brought the pond back to life. I told her
with conviction that I had never before dated a Ph.D.
in philosophy. She countered with something equally general,
that she had never before witnessed a professor of mathematics
express himself so fully in an almost unlawful
estuary. I began to cry. She comforted me far into the night.

TROW HILL, VERMONT

Death now like some long pardonable yellow strand
of hair—*well, that's okay, not*
a ramshackle American bomber smudging out
over Vesuvius the very night
of my birth, a cold rainy April night, just
about midnight and my grandfather
on the porch leaving an open can of tuna
for a stray cat my aunt
found frozen to the granite hitching post
at sunrise. It was a long war; thank god
for a newborn and bourbon in the morning's coffee.

THE NINE SOLITARY PLASTERS OF A COMEDY

...come i Roman per l'esercito molto, l'anno del giubileo,
su per lo ponte...

    Dante Alighieri

1

The pilgrims, delayed on the bridge, dream
with the cows scratching ribs against two fir trees...
a tablet, an old board with a fresh plaster
of ground bone, horse and rat, anniversary
of the red brass stylus making cones
of weird accents, angels
with brilliant foreheads and large ears,
Giotto asking if it was the ugly baby
who farted, Beatrice
decomposing under a June sun, haystacks
burning off on the hillside

like cantos...

Dante runs a stylus
through a wet plaster of bone
the ninth hour to vespers... all comedy
needy of serial cartoons of slate
waxed with sun, composing in bone, a sulfur rain
without benefit of notes... then he's
also dead & gone.

2

It was like that, winter slats
seconds apart. The cook wearing socks
on his breasts he could cut
chops from the lamb, yes salted

for legatees and popes most of them
stationed in Hell with worms for curls
bawling at the turquoise soprano wired to the ceiling.

The army of the horizon speaks in Greek,
then in Latin—he cooked first
for the brothel in Florence and then for
the army that spoke French when bargaining
for women who needn't cook lamb.
Full centuries of it. Just like that! Shit!
Crushed cinnabar, the red mineral & more sulfur.
The very complex afterlife of a small bee box, winter slats
seconds apart… *a small bee box and quinces on each yellow mark…*

3

The children being led through fog
in purple and green shrouds. The ghost
of a woman sitting there
so dead she seems
not to be naked. He wakes
with her hair in his mouth, a mistake
of selves… last night's wine off
the shelf. The cold rain of Provence
washes her body warm like piss.
Frogs falling out of the cumulus. All the foxes
of the district with mange
like the fallen boudoir sofas of Clement.

4

The three mouths of Lucifer
speaking at her forehead: Greek,
of course, Latin hallucinating
French with gutturals of purple grapes. The cook
speaks Italian to the mice—necks broken,

flies at the eyes and mouth.
The cook is stirring blood noodles, 3½ years to the false moon,
hot plasmas spooling off our sun
struck (*one potato, two potato*) on the occluded side. The jet
of platinum flame in the icy lecture hall
on a revolving cue ball. Laughter.
The gypsy elder in a Ravenna teashop
whispering to the fat cop
he's from 4 years in the future. Laughter. Again,

the bishop's fresh radish plate of noodles
with boiled eels.

5

Too late. Dante with a sack of gold dust scolding
legatees and circumadjutants
& their women with yellow wire brushes scouring their pale backs...
Dante now yelling irrevocably at the women,
'the fresh troops from Arezzo and Pisa will be slain by morning'—
the graves not dug for weeks!
The *maestro* now folding like the sunset
the many blankets infected with smallpox. He looks
at the arias leaping from their foreheads, their pendulous breasts
red with the work. Now even Hell has its supper bell.

6

Many white hands like leaves reaching out of the darkness
that *che il tacere è bello* (her body, unsayable)
a dignity of conifers along the horizon—
evil words issuing from the very few abstract men
who wear the simple wimple. *Beatrice. Then. Beatrice.*
The cold fog returning with the children, one shroud
almost radiant. He looks up at the cook with disgust
'the politics is much easier than the women.'

7

Dante dreams the orchard ladder is slimy
with chalk and snails. The chalklime was there to poison them.
The old cook praying to Jesus to forgive him…
a quick sunrise and Dante wakes with fever… a breeze lifting
    the curtains
as if beseeching him '*che il tacere è bello.*'

The mother counting coins in her blue apron
smiles like the sky and evaporates. The fever,
he believes, is abating. In the shadows the future pastor
St. John, pissing against the wall of Diogenes that crosses the
    scholar's room,
is holding another candle to the morning. *And the fucking*
exile begins again…

*

The hawk's beak dipped in snow for the quelling
of himself alone. With the apple tree
as the first and last notary. The seal
is stem and the spiral worm
that is rain-wrapped about it. A whole stem
that follows to its female gasket.
And an electric birdcage hanging by a thread. The fat cop
interviewing with Guelf mind the irritable bowel
of Clement *five,* dead now
to the obvious temptations that might be a child's drawing
on a window of early morning frost: the numb finger
a broken pencil. Macaroni boiling in the loft.
The child's portrait of himself as hawk.

8

The manuscript buried in the cupboard wall,
the urine steam of a manger,
the rose is a moving diagram

of *should,* not *always.* Love
generalized across a naked shoulder,
the shoulder generalized across another's,
baptized, in the moment, a bare leg
gently falling to the floor. **Laughter.**

9

        & more laughter. The
doves rising in morning light.
The light falling to the earth
as plaster to the boards. A poet's
brass pencil, hand shaking,

the simple collection of nails
making passion, ink and a blood-
soaked linen. Virgins with lamps
spending dumb light on them.
A silent mewing of cows and shepherds
in more simple adoration.

        The sun sinking also...

SNOWDEN IN HONG KONG

Ergo-gangs are raping the seafarer Bernadette
in the blue clay field,
sparks flying from the mouth of the night bear
where Istanbul is washed in riversongs
of men punished before, during, and after judgment,

or is this just Aquinas bloodied, peeing
in arcs into the darkest brush bucket—
canaries made of yellow sugar on the tree branch,
a woman weeping into an open sandwich;

the children have thrown gasoline back at the militia
with fat ponds of crying-gas to drown in,
a new moon begins its search of integers
like belief crossing the burning night streets. These numskulls

never had to cheat at canasta, their lives
replete with dead Greeks,
their bodies being washed in fragrant oils
by the mystery thieves of data. It was slavery then, Aquinas,
with prawns and gongs, *it was wrong then, you bastards—*
it was sundown in Hong Kong.

CLOAKED IN NIGHT, RISING IN RADIANT ORCHARD

A Ghost Story

1

The resin-orange house burned most of the evening
under the gibbous moon
with white laterals of galaxy
up in the linden tree
set apart from the house
so that it wouldn't attract lightning
and the very calamity
that is just now visiting house, barn,
and all the ladders from the orchard
leaning against them
like a red and black scaffolding
of large burning box.

This is the recurring dream
with an empty marble ballroom
and one large mirror: a naked woman
reflected in it in empty space—
she seems to be screaming silently
back at the gulls
circling over the crates of rotten peaches.

Sunlight dreams this just as an old clerk
breathing very slowly...   says
it is the egg clock
ticking against the milk cupboard.

The smoke is up in the trees
like *6's* of galaxy
and how can waking from this dream
be the first speech of a terrible
evening. *How can it be believed?*

2

for Philip Seymour Hoffman

The ghost of the old clerk left
the burning house to sit under the darkening tree, powders
of heroin
drifting across his stocking feet, the smoke
moving up the peninsula,
Andromeda stalking the ash way, *a trick*
of 6's, heroin rising
above his knees, the Maine coast
has been like this for centuries—
baskets from the Orient, stopped
he thinks with the rose paraffins of Cathay. A perfect
pyramid of snow now
in the lap. *He laughs...*

3

There is a triangle of burning rags and a cigar
in a silver tray. The wallpaper peeling into the flooded tub.
The blue jay leaves the branch
and the house is waking for its
last day.
There will be no supper bells...

If it's summer
in the barn, the fire cats
are boxed in the burning hay,
there is an occult alphabet
learned by ship captains, written
in slate above the asphalt stanchions.

There are cows running
into the pond. There's an alphabet of cows
standing in pond. The sky

is described in long barley dust and urine…

    4

My father's house has many rooms
with many mansions in them…
And the old icebox doors were lined
with zinc, chalk, and white cork.

The orchard trees are dancing
in their bare knees. A compound sentence
of Longinus touches sun
changed by smoke an infant's tooth
becomes a mustard seed of yellow fat and soot.

The brass pendulum of clock is
now so hot it stops
for the first time in centuries
of announcing an illusory house
to itself.

    5

It is the firstborn exploring alone
at the town dump, gulls
screaming above him, the small boy climbs into the old icebox,
everything rolling
in a descent through peaches, the door latching shut,
this is a hell
of the old orient. *It is the dream.*
They will
not find him until the early spring.

6

In the sinister agreement of the leaves,
in dark canvas sheaf,
the moon in disbelief
shifts its *p's & q's*—

he washes his hands
in kerosene.

Too much boxed scene, too much
in amber isinglass proof. Here
death is the mother of death.

You can tell
the dead in sleep for so few
are ever wearing shoes.

Waldo paints his wife nude
but standing in the bark and tack
webbing of her hunting cap.

Over her shoulder in the mirror
her figure is removed, more
kerosene and shoes,
but a large white goose flies through
the cold room. The marble
of the mouth is open to the wing.

The exorcist of italics says
to us
the fruit falling through the trees
will never be bruised...
the great hammocks of ash reaching up as carpeting...

7

The gamesman at his cold noon supper
careless with a dustpan
with a dead mouse and smoldering cigar...
The rich painter just back
from Tunisia. The drum
of goatskin placed almost
without ceremony on his son's empty coffin.

On the floor
the small orange hose, the tourniquet of knots with millimeters
of white laxative and lavender chalk—a packet
with the powders and it is

8

a sallow 1% solution, agreeing through that bank
of billiards, *the esthétique*
of disease she screams
at the lightning rods
like a giant fish spine down the clay roof,
the fire jumping whole barns,
the small chapel wall collapses
revealing
great wedges of green ice, calving
in the North Atlantic:

It is a dream in mist of lifeboats
filling with furs and diamonds
even the bilge like a pendulum
of waterclock
that also must now stop.

It is the dream with a woman:
screaming,

apples falling through the trees.

SCION, *CIRCA* TEN

I feel like a spent clerk
tramping away from the hillsides.
The camel sick
with blood in its urine.
It's the mystery of drunken birds
up in the morning date palms...
More and more intrigue
and cold lamb with raisins.

In recent memory
it's the waltz of the nutcracker
and a green
model-t backfiring...   in Damascus,
your mother's grave
filling in waves
during the late evening dust storm.

A tintype of a blue and rouged
pilot whale being fed alewives
from a yellow rowboat quickening everything—

it is dragging you away
from your sister's children
playing in ashes
while her dead husband carves the lamb.

The earthquake killed
a third of the government's cloaked men,
it arrives in the air
like prophecy
or a cocktail of naphtha
and English gin,

the birds
go drunken
and you stand in the doorway
spread-eagle
as if in a painted crucifixion
of a dead girl flummoxed in the tree.

ZONE

A flag utterly bleached with years of sun,
seemingly made thin with turpentine, is
an achievement in the yard of yellow grass.
Even the sun itself has faded
setting in the bee tenement of bearded palms.
The flag, nearly detached from its pole,
is somehow rioting with the wind.

This is just the first of six months of heat
and already a neighbor has been found
dead on his patio with a revolver
of glassy obsidian fallen to his sandals.
He told the maintenance man in the afternoon
he believed *those bees were wasps*
and they,
they were going to attack him and his tea, flying
like zeros right out of the sun
that will have blinded him.

John said the lawn mowers prevented him
from understanding what else he said, the face
truly reddening with the small success of evening.

THE CONVERGENCE

after Joost de Jonge

Yes, it is
the neglect of solids, not the potato
or significant pea, but the sphere
of neglect that is unconscious belief in sky.
An emigrant from the wild plateaus
who calls his hat, *sky?*

Now, Madame Cézanne is a potato. The painter
sits blinded among smoking heaps of sugar.
A German cash register ringing in the ear.
It is not the work of the dead
to clean the painter's shoes,
but, yes, the jealous rage
over the dark laces: *eternal, infinite eights, etc.*

Early spring, the many eyes in the room
turning into frogs' eggs, the cold pond
saying the photoelectric sun will one day
kill most of us with its kiss
while still struggling to adjust
her darkening paisley bonnet.

LA LOGIQUE ASSASSINE

circa 1919

The long memory, spirals in a night sky—
cold and focused
taking her shit in plato's cave—
the newspapers like living rock
have a last question, are forever, or...
scattered; red twine
bundles like stacks of folded trousers

in some future workcamp beside a river.
(One of Man Ray's girlfriends,
the suspicious blonde, scratching
a small shadow of breast—
should have been enough,
she muttering, *fuck-that*
the simple flirty) sonnet.

IV

THE COLOPHONS OF SOLOMON

> —the philistines with the inhabitants
> of Tyre; Assur also is joined
> with them: they have holpen, the children
> of Lot.
>
> Psalm 83:7–8

1

These simple trees along the Euphrates
are burning—
each leaf a sick duplicate
of methane, not some wink
of iris in an oil slick but the eye
of a bird lengthening in the brain, links
in a train of peacock flame
running between a sandy marsh
and the very dirty river
where Constantine's mother, Helena,
is bathing...

reason enough to peer across the night
to the telegraph at the St. Martin farm
sputtering to the stars and mule stockade
thinly stretched in mind
where a Queen

looks up to her red tunic in the trees:
a kind of blindness
she ascribes
to her old ambassadors of pantomime,
beating their camels
in a sudden rain
just outside the walls of Babylon.

2

The tents were striped beige and red,
each with the phantom stain of an armless woman
urinating in a stand of poplars—
a folding of ammonia and violet tincture
accidentally printing each huge canvas
then the average values of spirit gum
then burial in the vaults by the blockhead Wilson
against the next influenza outbreak
that didn't...   faces of greyhounds
laughing at the gun in climbing red dust.

3

The tents sold to a French athletic club in D.C.
who sold them to nudists, in Maine,
who collect every August
at the Popham breakers—
the glass trays of summer beer
and lemonade balanced
on the blond heads of waiters bobbing through dunes
to the smell of burnt venison, pepper-dulse seaweed and clams
reaching now the town's lifeguards standing
in harpoon boats against the Popham undertow,
their arms folded over big chests
with wilting penises. Cigars clearing the air
of mosquitoes and the baton's motion—
then the sudden covering of screaming gulls
over a lighthouse keeper's boat dumping bait
into the headwaters of the boiling Penobscot

and the Atlantic Ocean.

4

The war tax, the Queen
said, etches, *everywhere:*
the slaughter of water buffaloes,
her sad ministers in rain,
and the weeping grooms of the animals
who were smoking great flanks of meat
for a hillside of women and children
who had not eaten yet that winter. It

etches, also, *here*
in river's mist
with tracers and howitzers cooling
in the emptying night air, a diaphragm
of grapes and corn
in the fat stamps of earth

around a fallen Jerusalem.

5

The Red Cross station is grimly boarded up,
a checkpoint,
abandoned twice, mad Nepalese eating pie
where the glacier must interrogate its dead dog
in the green vapors of a terminal moraine.

The poor dog
being questioned repeatedly about an afterlife

and those dark Cathar banquet tables—
what his mother remembers
of the temporary morgues in the middle school
along *what* burning river?

6

Arab fishermen outside the auditorium
are smoking cigarettes
given to them by the French surgeon
whose family vanished in a dull cataract
of hot sand

this last September,

the rennet jelly-bomb
waking the father
who was sleeping in a clean
neighborhood theater. The ether jars,
knives, and wet sheets
all hanging in the pressing yellow air
that snakes in and out of the broad window
with a ricochet of night
that is the only lamp of projection,
a new matinee, a very
old light.

7

So the two witnesses
wrote in Greek
that there were hard walls of rain
breaking on Mt. Carmel
down to the baths and tunnels of Solomon
rising faster now
near the filthy sandstone skirts of Megiddo.

A drowned child
grasping a headless fox
shooting from the pipe stone
into the weak arms
of scrubbed cactus.

Pigeons dying of dry cough
down in the low
pomegranate grove.

8

This is where the dark prisoner
is kept in a hot plasma well
that is nearly bottomless. It was capped
with a ceramic formula,
with the wall of a collapsed
Byzantine church, more earth,
and then the donkey carrion in long iron braids.

The Mother's crocodiles sit in purple skirts
drawing the daily compass
of black and red gunpowder—

sky-walking women
of the catacombs filing their teeth to points,
the spray of the jelly-bomb
now tatting their dull paper gowns.

9

The Roman soldier, Gaianus, and five
Greek women holding sacks of pearls
were running from the stone granary
to the black skins of their tents.
The Roman is a giant. All five pagans
are *both* widows and virgins.

They are spending their treasure
to build a chapel floor
for the coming anchoress's Son
with her eight faces of tortured cubes

heaving under millenary tesseracts
of the ceramic circle
with two sea bass
fat from the depot ponds of the Jordan.

Ezekiel saying the ice storm
down the mountain-slopes
moved like a mussel shell that cleans
the coat from the dead kid. A blade of wind
that just lifted all the goats up,
then tumbling them into the sea
where they moved
like contrasting beans in boiling water.

10

Folded in the rain were
the dead golden songbirds of a boy-Judge. Apollo?
The insects in his beard
singing with the lips of hierophants, of giraffes,
of the sixth virgin of Antioch
riding her three-legged dog
that even the Sumerians dreamt of,

dreams beaten down from sky
by colored rugs
with iron burr and glass pleats
for a perfect conversion to suffering
on the waxy white plateau at Damascus.

11

In the winter garrisons
they are tossing bones against
that satan-dyxx and a rose-colored cloud
is moving over the green desert

just behind them. The American war tax
has increased twice this season...

In the winter garrisons...

12

Helena, in sunlight, peeling her orange,
needs her son's barber who sings.

The drunken Russians
in bear costumes:
those dead visitor giants sprawling
on pallets—   dead dressing
storms across the Pleiades.
His new tax on raisins and salt
telling her to sell on strength
in Algeria and on Mars—
these very flat planes of Ur; magical cubes
packing triangles
like snake spirals nesting in radiant sticks—
a blind holy man in marsh-jihad,
A'aru, *'djed* singers and the last light of Gir.

13

There is no simple algorithm of sticks
with black and white snakes in it
that packs Durga's cube
like a brain hemorrhage,

and then suddenly they ran
from the stone tanks
and the constructing of the ceramic cap
to their collapsing tents. The Roman
was something of a giant,

dead birds folded in his yellow beard—
He was once
the slough of a German wood.
No light
and dead deer curing
up high in the spruce.

14

Smoke, white with the chalk of the potter's chimney,
circling the ghosts of the executed Al-Hallaj
riding the spotted hogs and chariots
through the Vatican's walk-in cupboards

devoted to instruments of torture,
maps of the underworld,
and the Hamong'og's half-loaf of bran
that has cleared whole lines of priests
all the way back to the fey gloom
of the earliest synods...

back, in fact, to when the potato
was the most poisonous legume
of the highest penitent;
Saint Jerome feeding them
only to the dogs
and a tawny-colored lion
who brought the wood in for fires.

15

And *save our ships*—   the crise d'Octobre,
& *z stigma*—

an American radio announces 111 miners
drowned in West Virginia,

an oblivion-wall of motel bibles
broke, washing past them
with a naked canary rouged at the ankles
singing Shaker arias:

For the exegetes of coal, the exegetes
of snow...

it is the moon of changes.

16

They have executed Al-Hallaj
for biting Caesar's coin with suspicion
on the shaded orchard hill inside Babylon:
He'll die twice—   previously
in a dark Scythian salt mine flushed with rain:

one green angel in a ruby choker
laughs tin-bells-of-martyrdom
over the corpse of the black shia,
sufi, born of the Shim-woman,
zoroastrian afterbirth characteristic

offal of dying angels.

17

Your dream of the sandy flanks
of a large lion
pissing blood into the chest cavity
of satan's anonymous son, or

in a hilltop fog
two men with shortened hair
are seen stepping from a boat

onto the sea
turning now with the wind
and the drowning of the goats.

Aketous, in ruin, with the clock of oblivion
and a gypsum table.

The glass clepsydra of the scholars
of one candle
at the Steklov Institute, in Russia,
prophesying
Emperor Constantine's edict of AD 313
allowing his mother to worship freely
'the jesus'
across the tea and camel kingdoms
    of his leeward grace...

   18

...take right and two lefts,
bank is there
with billboard of winter. Two smokestacks,
and red hydro plant...

heaps of earthquake glass...

    ...faces of greyhounds
laughing at the gun; the rising dust...

in the rising red dust
of the big sun setting—
    feces of the greyhounds, running...

CopperCanyonPress.org

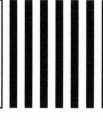

BUSINESS REPLY MAIL
FIRST-CLASS MAIL   PERMIT NO. 43   PORT TOWNSEND WA

POSTAGE WILL BE PAID BY ADDRESSEE

Copper Canyon Press
PO Box 271
Port Townsend, WA 98368-9931

NO POSTAGE
NECESSARY
IF MAILED
IN THE
UNITED STATES

What do you think?

BOOK TITLE: _____

COMMENTS: _____

_____

OUR MISSION:

Poetry is vital to language and living. Copper Canyon Press publishes extraordinary poetry from around the world to engage the imaginations and intellects of readers.

Thank you for your thoughts!

Can we quote you? ☐ yes ☐ no

☐ Please send me a catalog full of poems and email news on forthcoming titles, readings, and poetry events.

☐ Please send me information on becoming a patron of Copper Canyon Press.

NAME: _____

ADDRESS: _____

CITY: _____ **STATE:** ____ **ZIP:** ____

EMAIL: _____

MAIL THIS CARD, SHARE YOUR COMMENTS ON FACEBOOK OR TWITTER, OR EMAIL POETRY@COPPERCANYONPRESS.ORG

Copper Canyon Press
A nonprofit publisher dedicated to poetry

19

The sweet pink-and-black snake
speaking in whispers to the decapitated saint
about prisoners in a sulfur mine
farther down the desert peninsula. How the dark bread

made with sawdust, yellow chaff, and kitchen paste
must be crumbled between fingers
first,
and then only *slowly* eaten. Saving
the blood in your mouth for painting
the dead conifer on the ridge.

20

Beside the tapped Saudi well
the gray sedan is burning.

Paula and the French surgeon, Moreau,
are sipping blackish hill tea, saying, "emotion is
a kind of money."

All afternoon they wanted to purchase
parachute silk from syphilitic crusaders,
to drape over the berths in the night train
to Acre.

The conductor, strutting the aisles
of the sleeper cars, crying—
Alarm. Exeunt. Ptolemy is hiding in your dreams
with piles, and an eggshell scalp;
without a ticket or any purple stamp on his papers.

He is out of the beer garden, sad and fibbing to women
about the migration of fleas and planets.

Now, friends, we'll never speak of him
again.

    21

Except for their visit to the Popham breakers
while she shows her breasts to him
as if in some open prejudice
that is
the invention of oceans. Ishmael

Moreau coughing blood into his millennial sandwich.

Paula's hair standing
in that first half-second of rennet fire—
her dead child, a jewel,
broken bodies
like semicolons, and the actual
standing orchards of pomegranate.

    22

It would seem hydrogen
is their lesson. In the apostasy
of local onion fields that surround the mound
in its small prison and dig,
the jailer with parking tickets from Haifa
reads new coded briefs: 'stego-stitch,'
'quelled river,' and 'white noise.' The simplest
instruction: & scriptural,

Write what you see, clearly/
and further/
with the legs of a table/
so they may read it, and then run.

23

So Ishmael said to his daughter, it is
a good time to say goodnight
to tonight. Yes
what started the greyhounds running
was the bomb, not the painted gun.
It is a method
that can be relied upon,
the use of the one now as common
as the other below darkening palms.

The popcorn scattered everywhere in the grandstand—
the torn tickets, at least
half of them, caught in a large purple storm
down at the kennels and the St. Martin farm.

I feel increasingly that we have been written
entirely out of the prophecies. But not the lottery—

Us and that Virgin with a three-legged dog?
The tortoise scab on his back and her sack
of pearls. Not the farm?

24

Abraham speaking softly to his son,
Ishmael, about a giraffe butchered by a Christian mob
in the Beirut zoo—
how its roasted tongue still went the length
of a picnic table with Christian and Muslim
children eating it from starvation...

The figs in the basket have worms that will reject
the slingshot maneuver around the moon
down the long intestine into a sunbeam. They will
lodge there like bureaucrats who are too happy

to embrace salvation:

The soteriological a-cardinality of the numbers, the prisoner
trits digging a cartesian well for hot air.
That's what Abraham means. This is the un-guessed

nightlife of an antichrist. The progressive
perfect orgasm with your false teeth *in*
and your legs *up...*   the heathen and missionary
positions with eye-contact and bats flapping.
The method is not the gun, not a cannon,

but a big red sun, asking
where's Uncle Samuel?
Has he gone to the dogs again, forgetting
these poor children? At Nagasaki?

At Washington?

25

110°, 119°, the American radio,
west of the Rockies, the air
at twilight
skipping in pellucid ponds of light
and the female caller-in from Tucson
says: Mom, I'm watching them
and one-fifth of these folks
walking over the border are straight
from Pakistan: islamo-fascists with humble hats,
egg crates, blankets, the skin
of a donkey with bullet holes in it
and I bet it's yellowcake
in the middle of those mud-bricks.
Mom, it's

26

happening all over again. What really pisses me off
is the way at night they steal my laying hens—
they're a cross between a mongoose
and the south end of a mule. Easy, easy
targets; but I guess their babies got to eat.

I watch the wildfires up in the hills
like a goddamn television.

Twice now I have dreamt that I see
hundreds of them, naked and huddled together for warmth
in a dark, *arroyo-*
givin-box-canyon. It starts to rain.
A lot of them are screaming. Mom says
that Bill Clinton is an evil one and so too
his women.

Mom announced at church
that she saw Rudy G. in a pretty dress
rising like some Voodoo queen
from the very belly of New York City
and he was distributing coupons
for Ivory Soap. Mom's gonna vote for him,
twice, or so she hopes.

27

The Papal envoy crosses the levee struts
a crow turning away
suddenly with the wind
his white scarf falling
to the water, the priest
stoops, retrieving
not his scarf

but absentmindedly
the remnant of cloud
no longer reflected there, nor
in the burning oil drum, burning river,
hubcap with rainwater, ceramic
hubcap of the satan-dyxx
boarding the tanker in New Orleans
for the future mustard districts
of Cairo.

(thunderbolt vehicle, Yeshe O'd
and his thousand-year-old
pack of hunting greyhounds.)

OM MANI PADME HUNG

28

The pink fretted cloud above the mountain pass,
a sleek Chinese train breaking
like waves over the junk plateau.
American cosmocrats, landed bureaucrats
and academics sucking in
little sprigs of blood in their guts.

The dogs are stretching ahead of the speeding train,
the train is burning. Tibetan horsemen
are gaining from the southwest.
They call to their dogs
running now in a local hailstorm
with the sun
stunning like the ice itself.
O'd says, "we must learn to love these Chinese—

their green caps will chatter"
down past the mound and its baths, past

the ruined walls of Jerusalem
to its suburbs
where they are dynamiting the gardens
to bury thousands of Russian dead
from the quakes and battlefields...   dark

little secret policeman, *cheka ghost,*
with a fetid beanpole emerging at the collarbone,
you too are dead.

29

93°, west of Chicago: well, Ted,
the light is shooting from the clouds
down the gulch.
Ted, I guess I am no first caller-in,
not this time, Samson. When those Arab munitions
blew up and started the greyhounds running
without a gun; well, Ted, the ground moved
beneath those poor dogs, many stumbling. Ted, I ask myself

would those local desert folks
really tolerate gambling on dogs. Mom says they will
gamble on dogs, fine horses, camels,
and even pigs. Well, I'm not
really sure about the pigs...

that bomb was powerful and dusted with something—
those dogs stumbling
'cause the ground was moving beneath them:

30

Ted, if one of these radical Arabs does nuke
a city in the U.S.A.; well, then, Mom says
we'll nuke 'em right back. All those Axis countries, and a few

others thrown in for *simple slim pickins...*

Mom says
this will be the end of any hen
laying an egg ever again? My question
for the professor is,

does *mom* have something there
for a fact?
or is she pulling my legs
while snappin' my bra back?

31

The Queen has found the birthplace of Jesus
and the tomb. The soldiers,
long-quartered with her, joke
Constantine dropped some datura in her soup.
The foxes braying and barking in the hills
while her diggers find the hard-

straw and tar-manure from the manger wall.
It burned along with most of Bethlehem
two evenings after the crucifixion.
Shepherds, that early morning, saw
a half-moon fall to the earth
and a burning man-dog
run into the desert marl and scrub.

Helena, bathing in the long depots, spoke
in a voice that convinced her guards
she was no longer human. And
they prayed to be forgiven for their jokes.

Weeks later they were found hanging in the orchard.
Where they remain in carbon dolmens

until summer ponds freeze over
from Spain to Manchuria.

    32

Queen Helena saying
that Gaianus had finished
the work before her son's birth

cobbling up a granary wall
near the old mound not far
beyond the gas crypt
dug from salt for the satan-dyxx…

Ishmael has brought back his father's
printed tents from a Grange Hall,
near Bath. He has now
presented them, in Gaza,
to the Vatican envoy, Father Maite,
who is just now
divining the squatting woman
shamelessly chemical on every tent.
The refugees of this new city
insist there is nothing there

and laugh pointing at the priest,

hoping for a long, dry, and musty sleep
in a harsh November midnight…

    33

Ennio and Etna are the twins. Though their mother
watched ghosts in blue pajamas
fly above the orchards in Vinci. The light
gaining sacks of sand as she bicycles
through the evening rain.

The twins have only known the West Bank. They're studying
an armless woman who's squatted among young trees.
Yellow and purple like an old bruise, the tents—
Etna tells Moreau—are like sulking elephants. The doctor laughs.

Ennio says, no,
they're aunt's loaves of raisin bread;
and the sunlight is snow—

34
The snow has been pissed on by elephants.
The locust are dead.

The young widow passing the twins with her pails of water
looks to Ennio. He runs down the hill
to his mother. The Evil-eye
on roller skates

zooms past them under the green awning
into the open kitchen
of the dead bomb-maker, Jamal,
who died in a flash fire
while melting boxes of crayons for his daughters
given to them
by a Christian charity from Rome.
There are handkerchiefs and American dollars
on the table. The twins' laughter again,
two violins in D-minor. The evil-eye swimming
out of the upstairs window in a narrow bundle of colors.
The twins' mother spitting into the air. A black-
and-tangerine fire.

35

Moreau, the widower, would adopt the twins
and their mother.
But the children cry when wind
turns the pages of their silver Koran.

The mother cries when the doctor
holds her hand.

36

The three horsemen are collapsing
on the ridge in a cloud of orange locust
with the tomato fat of lamb
or chicken, the horses rolling on their backs,
wings like wire-mesh lacerating,
grilling with static combs
the wide-open eyes of the stallion.

(The old man picks his nose, saying,
the mirror has fallen into the Indian Ocean
polluting with the acids of wormwood
a third of Earth's water—
Houston demurs, 'the Soviet *Mir* was covered
in a black galactic fungus
that eats manganese and aluminum.')

The three horsemen who presumed
to judge a black sufi saint
are now on their backs
wiggling in a storm of insects that know no hesitation
leaving holes where the septum was—

little put-put *in,* put-put *out,*
little *cheka* policeman,
this is your late-afternoon oblivion.

There's no gun to talk about.

37

Someone said to Jesus,
that the clothes of the dead were worn
to the wedding. He said,
"be happy for them, they'll be naked again."

38

The fox nested in limousines.
Boxes that nested in
shadow tesseract, in a crypt
booming in the sand elevator
where the dyxx was, at last, fixed.

The Rabbi who is saying the Book
will never be finished. Fall
on your feet. Messengers

are crossing
just beneath the ceramic table.
The nuns
said that the two observers
were prisoners also
and they rotated in large cubes of blue wool.

Rabbis sweeping the prayer house. The donkey skin
is on the roof of knives.

The Rabbi smiles and says, "when it gets like this,
Doctor, I think of that pink rat-shit,
Shake-spear, at his morning rehearsals—
a kick of my boots in thanks
to a God who doesn't repeat himself."

39

The flooded plain of wagons, farmers
raising rakes against a warlord
dressed in paper paisley; the starter's gun
should imbibe corn & teeth
in the white back of the brain. But a

jelly-roll of fertilizer and kerosene
did the trick with the open sleeve
of blood and rain.

40

So the warlord and the Vatican priest are dead.
A piece of cloud rising from the smaller body.
Dogs broken on the lawns—
anthrax in two days, general across the valley. And then
stopped. The brutes in Damascus
knew the warhead when they saw it
in prayer.

Glass suborning the thistle stylus
on a phonograph one cranks.
Bye-bye, blackbird. Morning sky. The sweet manna
of the water tanks and a crypt
burst open at the gum plug
where the ideal solid
is the orange root
with an inscription of three stars, dovetail

& frontispiece. The cisterns
are below the mount. Firepond
against a mercy seat gone wrong...

41

Far outside the suburbs of Tel Aviv
the failed Iranian rocket
leaves a radio haze along the horizon
and then midway a Ferris wheel
with black bears seated in it
flies from the axle-cog
landing in the sea. The lights
of the Ferris wheel leave afterimages
in the night sky:
We know this script:

Elegant, *Mohammedan.* This is how it happens.
Everyone listening. Everything stopped.
The long verse stops
like the giraffe's tongue
rolled with a stake through it, baked
there in the park. Life's like this.

You shouldn't say so,
shouts the lilac—the big head lowers in the rain,
green and gray submarines leaving the coastline
of Maine where at land's end
the people are naked and crying into their hands.
They were a colony.
They are naked by ambition. It was a first step.
No one paid any attention.
The beginnings and the ends,
Mad Solomon said, "the putting on of nakedness
is for the dead."

42

An artesian water-gig volunteering in the evening's mustard:
the dustfall of cowflies, stooped
and complicated by light—

small girls in yellow rags are
leaving the thousand years of a dry hillside;
the earth moves

lifting the children into the sky,
to the poor kitchens of the darkening mountain
where hungry birds in their least bright aspect

                                                              reply

in generous laughter-like repetitions of flight...
it is again

                    the mother night.

ELEGY FOR BRIAN YOUNG

On the TV the clearing images
with rain are occasionally stirred
by the rotor-blades of black choppers:

the scene, one of five major gyres
of garbage on our high seas—   landfill
with the bones of animals and humans
sorting out with closed turquoise
barrels of toxins like immortal turtles over
the complicated water and its chop...   they are,
with all others, searching for a mystery plane
that grabbed even you
like a common headline:

BRITISH AND AMERICAN GOVERNMENTS
LYING ABOUT TREBLE SEVEN:
over the black palms of Diego Garcia:
Jenny called last night
to say that last week
you passed with a smile
on your face that was also mysterious.

You know they used to put brilliantly light
children up in the violent crow's-nest
of big wooded galleons and even they would,
in their queer being,
be tossed by the pitching
into the difficult waters, then
only to be reeled back in
with the white waist-rope
if not actually halved by it in pink suds, sure

these kids *could* fly like this twice,
even three times in a single night.

This is where the good poet and friend
generally runs out of things to see, wanting almost
anything like, *let us say*, garbage
for as far as the eye *can* see,
the simple eternal hopefulness of facts
reversing in an almost gentle wind
(*We never did give a damn.* Did we?)

         across a stormy Indian ocean.

DELMORE SCHWARTZ VIGILANT AMONG
LARGE-HEADED LILACS

It is a scent that's tracked through mountain mist
down to the hillsides and the Jersey coast...
All your friends organized loosely
against you, huddling
there like the fat-headed flowers
nodding in their little disagreements
like boxes of soap and cereal
in the borrowed shopping cart with a broken wheel.
The hobo's acquisitions, at dawn, and you wanting
to remember what consolation
in men's magazines Proust
passed to Swann
with the Paris barbers shaking large aprons
full of human hair and teeth onto the streets.

You repeat
something about 'small frogs in small ponds'
and the editor from the *Partisan*
adjusts her left shoulder and brassiere
and you noticed only the steam
rising from the winter sewer.

You told her you were not confused
but that she might have been dead
for some months now. *From
the head up* is what you were thinking.

You said *if you're going to
shoot me*—make it any day but Tuesday.

The astrologer's great Cross written in sand
with a stick of poison sumac
and the smoking innards of lambs. An augury
of black tea and gunpowder.
Your dearest friends have always harbored
the darkest thoughts against you
and your empty bowery cupboards.

So what, dead from the neck down, is what
you said to *the Ex...*   about yourself.

How you were becoming silent, athletic
while signing with your hands. The vowel
of thumb and first finger
from the second baseman to the catcher
while he's rising from the knees, throwing
off his mask, spinning clockwise, dust
like mummy bandages around him, the head
way back, looking up and homeward,
cleats pivot on the sack...
You told her to fuck off, much too
complicated for most of us,
the crowd now silent and the stitched ball
falling into the grandstand
for the paying customers and their miniature children.

SPY

The woman in the red dress who runs
past me with a hemp sack full of tangerines
is just the membranous summer wind.
I pay her no attention.

In a world reflected in glass
even the mannequins
look back at me with suspicion,
and if they didn't
how could I trust them
walking their dogs on clear plastic leashes
under the swampy lindens.

The clown crossing the street with a makeshift
helium bouquet of condoms
is a middle-aged woman
who by smiling adjusts her yellowing dentures.
Her husband is the recently dead Czech dentist

that washed up in the river
with a living mask of young turtles
feeding from his worried visage.

She is rushing to the magistrate's house,
a lame stepson's ninth birthday.
They are all innocent is my first thought...

The counterfeit Seurat that hung
from the dead husband's surgery showed
a starving man with a trumpet, blue pixels
like a few hairs sprouting from the nostrils.

It is this figure even in memory
who must not ever be believed... back in the *Bar's* shadows
he is cutting heads off fish to bury
in his girlfriend's bank of roses, the conch
shell handle on her derringer
printed a faded skull
on the inside of her thigh, hair
falling over the eye sockets. She is innocent
also and a sloven.

I was disgusted on my third birthday by a bloody
triumph of swans in an ester fog
from swollen pitcher plants crossing the pond.
I was happy while digesting
my cucumber sandwich.
The man beside me on the park bench
asking, "What was Shakespeare's
last play?" It is odd
that even when Prospero lost his magic
he still didn't want his dukedom back.
I would never have trusted him,
not him,
not even on a simple errand for sherbert,
the box raspberry, the box lemon.

GOYA'S CLEANING WOMAN

The blue dates soak in the yellowing cream
and he says there is mathematics
in the Christmas chalk that is wiped off the slate
with rags rejected by the dressing stations.
There is a black mold in the crumpled lacecoat
with a faded impression of hummingbirds
slumped over with poise
like our Savior from the blasted tree.
If the hill is a skull then the flittering birds
are lice and eggs in the wig. Fog and
grave soil on the master's shoes. The sick horse
dragging the dory
through the canal water.
He folds rice paper into invisibility.

PROPHECY IN LIEU OF A LIEN

for David St. John

Wild turkeys nervously strolling through the ruined cemetery
have complained that the cold elevators in the tenement
across the street have in each dilapidated carriage-box
instructions in braille on large brass plates, dictating
lift without translation by weight in stones, balancing pans
with dark fists of turquoise in faded heaps painted
on the foyer wall by W.P.A. alcoholics with fresh loaves of bread
applied to a simple gravity of mural paint like Greek sponges
once donated as provision against starvation by a young Guggenheim
who drowned in conflict with a glacier. A painter with her skirt
tucked into an army belt has used a long knife to saw a turkey's
head off, its dead beard in the green frozen grass still talking
mostly in rapid objection to slaughter and the fashionable melancholy.

Comb and beard, souvenirs of the sunset while the physical sun
strangely rises like a bright headless bird that is collapsing
now on one of the wide ledges of a pink wedding cake
taller than the two Polish bakers standing on sanitary ladders,
the youngest is a blond unflummoxed and lanky long-distance runner
who did once dive for sponges on the crenellated seafloor—
*   occasionally*
he kept one, cutting it precisely into small custard-colored apples
which his high-school-aged lover with raven hair employed
as a method of contraception.

In sleep he would sometimes feel his penis nudge the sea sponge
and he would see wild turkeys nervously strolling around him.
Jews were detained in this cemetery before being loaded onto trains—
the woodbox of the locomotive sending puffs of steam against
the night air like polka dots of a future time even nearer still
to the mysterious river running gold and silver, even
*   nearer to the absolute*

countryside of postponed abject fear rendered in egg tempera
by a watercolorist who is suffering much of the day from trembling
and diarrhea, her mascara like polka dots on the horizon no longer
with several dusky deer in certain flight, no longer near...

KATHMANDU

Long brown monkeys are slow-dancing in fresh snow, all
six balancing red tennis balls
on their noses, the smoke from the broken stone
furnace and shrine a cloak
weighting them with hunger
like the quick mime of children.

The last tremor disturbed bells all along the north wall.

Monkeys are dancing in falling snow
which we know is ash
from a row of ruptured kilns—

the monkeys are drunk from the splitting
barrels of beer that are burning
behind the old hotel.

They were trained to the tennis balls
by a legless merchant
who is selling knives
when the clay roof's applause
crushes his back and skull
and the monkeys begin immediately their matinee for trekkers
whose favorite cousin is exchanging
snow for oxygen, now
the froth of blood for snow. The performance slowing

to the dead tourist's transistor
radio resting on cobble— silhouettes
walking before the lamps on the bridge,
the ghost voice of Roy Orbison
from the dropped radio

moving the solemn monkeys
through snow. Whole lifetimes

passing between aftershocks,
so numerous
they increase the drunkenness
of these cloaked animals just a gene splice
away from the humans who are now sleeping
in the ruins.

DECEMBER 7, 2015

1

Winter nights in the desert
are this cold? The furnace
silent because my throat
is already raw. It is
maybe 42° out...

And the cat jumps at me
for fun. I twist my ankle.
She then begins to study with questions
the leg like Robert's horse
beside the "lovely, dark and deep."

I say *if you must know*
I'm dying now of
exposure to a frozen bag of peas.
A red swollen ankle
our only source of heat. I laugh again.
If you must know...

Then, she immediately
falls asleep.

2

This morning after my father's death
I woke to a man
with a bluish blade,
who in the rigors of renewal
was dropping yellow sacks of dates
from the palm trees. I woke,

after all,
to a clear and felt winter light
that blessed even the streets
beneath the tall and metropolitan trees.

TWO ELOPING DISKS WITH THE SAME RADIUS

Euclid was alone at his poor supper. He witnessed
his two eyes wandering
to the point of collision, all of this
a simple reflection in a bowl of soup: the natural
triangle that worries itself
into the brow with strong oarsmen
pulling Euclid down the river that seems all wrong.

The rocking of the boat in the cold water
promises nausea—a white crane flying at night
impossibly low over them—he thinks, *shit,*
there must be some mistake.
There was vertigo and a fall in a stone tub.
An open-pit burial
with a red false flag of fish bladder.

He asked for a cake of blue thistle, being alone;
instead they gave him fog and a now-burning boat.
I said he was alone and you're asking *but what about*
those two oarsmen—well, you know
death is an unreliable narrator at ease
with the last arc minutes
of Mrs. Vesica Piscis, the great mother
who is alive within us all.
Smile. Please, smile. *I know.*

GHOST WRITER

The blue-and-white Cessna coughed out over the desert floor—
there is a blinking margin of starry night that's canal water.
A clumsy coyote descends an old hill of garbage. *Death is visiting
my friends.* No one is impressed any longer. Column inches of suns
in the stagnant water. Death, in fact, is shy and clumsy—looking
over its shoulder. The unscheduled slinking through a moon field
of vulgar agave and crushed shell-life that is some millionaire's
lost airstrip. The wife inside is happy and undressing—she sips
gin while the swamp cooler asks her to please finish that damn
crossword puzzle in Wednesday's newspaper: *reticule.
anathemata. divan. hemorrhage.* Her left hand releases
a very fat string of pearls. She is just now sleeping in a chair.
Not another human for hundreds of miles. And it is surely
a wonderful world. *perpendicular. charlemagne.* Light rain.
The cooling light from her husband's fish tanks.

Norman Dubie is the author of thirty books of poetry, including *The Quotations of Bone,* winner of the 2016 Griffin International Poetry Prize, as well as *The Volcano, The Insomniac Liar of Topo, Ordinary Mornings of a Coliseum,* and *The Mercy Seat: Collected & New Poems 1967–2001,* all from Copper Canyon Press. His poems have appeared in such magazines as *The New Yorker, The American Poetry Review, Narrative, Blackbird, Lake Effect, Bombay Gin, The Paris Review,* and *The Fiddlehead.* He is the recipient of many fellowships from granting institutions, including the John Simon Guggenheim Memorial Foundation, the Ingram Merrill Foundation, the Poetry Foundation (the Bess Hokin Prize), and the National Endowment for the Arts. Mr. Dubie received the PEN Center USA Literary Award for Poetry in 2002. He teaches in Tempe, Arizona, where he has lived these last forty years in an alkali desert, mostly in the company of cats.